CATCALENDAR

2011 ENGAGEMENT CALENDAR

Catalog No. H228

Published by Pomegranate Communications, Inc.
Box 808022, Petaluma CA 94975

Available in the UK and mainland Europe from Pomegranate Europe Ltd.
Unit 1, Heathcote Business Centre, Hurlbutt Road, Warwick, Warwickshire CV34 6TD, UK

© 2010 Judith Kamman Kliban
www.eatmousies.com / www.kliban.com

Pomegranate also publishes B. Kliban's work in wall, mini wall, desk, postcard, and coloring calendars for 2011, in a coloring book, gift wrap, gift enclosures, postcards, notecards, pop-up cards, holiday cards, a stationery set, a birthday book, an address book, bookmarks, posters, magnets, and the book *CatChristmas*. Other products and publications in our extensive line include a wide variety of specialty calendars, invitations, thank you cards, Knowledge Cards®, mousepads, and journals. For more information or to place an order, please contact Pomegranate Communications, Inc., 800 227 1428, www.pomegranate.com.

Dates in color indicate US federal holidays.
Dates listed for all astronomical events in this calendar are based on Coordinated Universal Time (UTC),
the worldwide system of civil timekeeping. UTC is essentially equivalent to Greenwich Mean Time.
Moon phases and American, Canadian, and UK holidays are noted.

 NEW MOON   FIRST QUARTER   FULL MOON   LAST QUARTER

One of the longest-running feuds in the cartooning world pits the cat people against the dog people. In one corner stand the champions of Snoopy, Fred Basset, and Pluto, while in the other we find the Garfield, Fritz, and Krazy Kat partisans. (Seldom does one encounter an artist equally at ease with both species; only *The New Yorker's* George Booth comes to mind.)

B. "Hap" Kliban (American, 1935–1990), like his fellow cat sketchers, was apt to dwell on the hedonism and the mischievousness of his subjects. But early in his career he also produced lovingly detailed realistic sketches of the cats who inhabited his studio, pictures that convey sloth and slumber without a hint of the demonic. The first collection of his art, simply entitled *Cat,* included some of these gentler pen and ink drawings, along with the cartoons that surprised and thrilled readers with a mordant, surreal wit.

We're calling this round a victory for the cat people.

2011

JANUARY

s	m	t	w	t	f	s
						1
2	3	4	5	6	7	8
9	10	11	12	13	14	15
16	17	18	19	20	21	22
23	24	25	26	27	28	29
30	31					

FEBRUARY

s	m	t	w	t	f	s
		1	2	3	4	5
6	7	8	9	10	11	12
13	14	15	16	17	18	19
20	21	22	23	24	25	26
27	28					

MARCH

s	m	t	w	t	f	s
		1	2	3	4	5
6	7	8	9	10	11	12
13	14	15	16	17	18	19
20	21	22	23	24	25	26
27	28	29	30	31		

APRIL

s	m	t	w	t	f	s
					1	2
3	4	5	6	7	8	9
10	11	12	13	14	15	16
17	18	19	20	21	22	23
24	25	26	27	28	29	30

MAY

s	m	t	w	t	f	s
1	2	3	4	5	6	7
8	9	10	11	12	13	14
15	16	17	18	19	20	21
22	23	24	25	26	27	28
29	30	31				

JUNE

s	m	t	w	t	f	s
			1	2	3	4
5	6	7	8	9	10	11
12	13	14	15	16	17	18
19	20	21	22	23	24	25
26	27	28	29	30		

2011

JULY

s	m	t	w	t	f	s
					1	2
3	4	5	6	7	8	9
10	11	12	13	14	15	16
17	18	19	20	21	22	23
24	25	26	27	28	29	30
31						

AUGUST

s	m	t	w	t	f	s
	1	2	3	4	5	6
7	8	9	10	11	12	13
14	15	16	17	18	19	20
21	22	23	24	25	26	27
28	29	30	31			

SEPTEMBER

s	m	t	w	t	f	s
				1	2	3
4	5	6	7	8	9	10
11	12	13	14	15	16	17
18	19	20	21	22	23	24
25	26	27	28	29	30	

OCTOBER

s	m	t	w	t	f	s
						1
2	3	4	5	6	7	8
9	10	11	12	13	14	15
16	17	18	19	20	21	22
23	24	25	26	27	28	29
30	31					

NOVEMBER

s	m	t	w	t	f	s
		1	2	3	4	5
6	7	8	9	10	11	12
13	14	15	16	17	18	19
20	21	22	23	24	25	26
27	28	29	30			

DECEMBER

s	m	t	w	t	f	s
				1	2	3
4	5	6	7	8	9	10
11	12	13	14	15	16	17
18	19	20	21	22	23	24
25	26	27	28	29	30	31

december

dec ▪ jan

30 | 364

NEW YEAR'S DAY HOLIDAY

31 | 365

NEW YEAR'S DAY

1 | 1

2 | 2

JANUARY

s	m	t	w	t	f	s
						1
2	3	4	5	6	7	8
9	10	11	12	13	14	15
16	17	18	19	20	21	22
23	24	25	26	27	28	29
30	31					

january

monday

3 | 3

tuesday

4 | 4 ●

wednesday

5 | 5

BANK HOLIDAY (CANADA, UK)

BANK HOLIDAY (SCOTLAND)

january

JANUARY

s	m	t	w	t	f	s
						1
2	3	4	5	6	7	8
9	10	11	12	13	14	15
16	17	18	19	20	21	22
23	24	25	26	27	28	29
30	31					

january

10
monday
10

11
tuesday
11

12
wednesday
12 ◑

january

JANUARY

s	m	t	w	t	f	s
						1
2	3	4	5	6	7	8
9	10	11	12	13	14	15
16	17	18	19	20	21	22
23	24	25	26	27	28	29
30	31					

january

17

18

19

january

JANUARY

s	m	t	w	t	f	s
						1
2	3	4	5	6	7	8
9	10	11	12	13	14	15
16	17	18	19	20	21	22
23	24	25	26	27	28	29
30	31					

january

january

thursday
27
27

friday
28
28

saturday
29
29

sunday
30
30

JANUARY

s	m	t	w	t	f	s
						1
2	3	4	5	6	7	8
9	10	11	12	13	14	15
16	17	18	19	20	21	22
23	24	25	26	27	28	29
30	31					

jan ▪ feb

february

LUNAR NEW YEAR

FEBRUARY

s	m	t	w	t	f	s
		1	2	3	4	5
6	7	8	9	10	11	12
13	14	15	16	17	18	19
20	21	22	23	24	25	26
27	28					

february

february

friday

◑ 11 | 42

saturday

12 | 43

sunday

13 | 44

FEBRUARY

s	m	t	w	t	f	s
		1	2	3	4	5
6	7	8	9	10	11	12
13	14	15	16	17	18	19
20	21	22	23	24	25	26
27	28					

february

monday

14

VALENTINE'S DAY

---

tuesday

15

---

wednesday

16

february

thursday

17 | 48

friday

○ 18 | 49

saturday

19 | 50

sunday

20 | 51

FEBRUARY

s	m	t	w	t	f	s
		1	2	3	4	5
6	7	8	9	10	11	12
13	14	15	16	17	18	19
20	21	22	23	24	25	26
27	28					

february

monday
21

PRESIDENTS' DAY

tuesday
22

wednesday
23

february

thursday

◑ 24 ₅₅

friday

25 ₅₆

saturday

26 ₅₇

sunday

27 ₅₈

FEBRUARY

s	m	t	w	t	f	s
		1	2	3	4	5
6	7	8	9	10	11	12
13	14	15	16	17	18	19
20	21	22	23	24	25	26
27	28					

feb ▪ mar

monday
28

tuesday
1

wednesday
2

march

MARCH

s	m	t	w	t	f	s
		1	2	3	4	5
6	7	8	9	10	11	12
13	14	15	16	17	18	19
20	21	22	23	24	25	26
27	28	29	30	31		

march

monday	
66	7

tuesday	MARDI GRAS
67	8 INTERNATIONAL WOMEN'S DAY

wednesday	ASH WEDNESDAY
68	9

march

thursday
10 | 69

friday
11 | 70

saturday
◑ ## 12 | 71

DAYLIGHT SAVING TIME BEGINS

sunday
13 | 72

MARCH

s	m	t	w	t	f	s
		1	2	3	4	5
6	7	8	9	10	11	12
13	14	15	16	17	18	19
20	21	22	23	24	25	26
27	28	29	30	31		

march

march

ST. PATRICK'S DAY

thursday
17 | 76

friday
18 | 77

PURIM (BEGINS AT SUNSET)

saturday
○ 19 | 78

VERNAL EQUINOX 23:21 UTC

sunday
20 | 79

MARCH

s	m	t	w	t	f	s
		1	2	3	4	5
6	7	8	9	10	11	12
13	14	15	16	17	18	19
20	21	22	23	24	25	26
27	28	29	30	31		

march

monday
21

tuesday
22

wednesday
23

march

SUMMER TIME BEGINS (UK)

MARCH

s	m	t	w	t	f	s
		1	2	3	4	5
6	7	8	9	10	11	12
13	14	15	16	17	18	19
20	21	22	23	24	25	26
27	28	29	30	31		

march

87 *monday*
28

88 *tuesday*
29

89 *wednesday*
30

thursday

31 | 90

friday

1 | 91

saturday

2 | 92

MOTHERING SUNDAY (UK)

sunday

● 3 | 93

APRIL

s	m	t	w	t	f	s
					1	2
3	4	5	6	7	8	9
10	11	12	13	14	15	16
17	18	19	20	21	22	23
24	25	26	27	28	29	30

april

monday

94 | 4

tuesday

95 | 5

wednesday

96 | 6

april

thursday

7 | 97

friday

8 | 98

saturday

9 | 99

sunday

10 | 100

APRIL

s	m	t	w	t	f	s
					1	2
3	4	5	6	7	8	9
10	11	12	13	14	15	16
17	18	19	20	21	22	23
24	25	26	27	28	29	30

april

101

monday

11

102

tuesday

12

103

wednesday

13

april

PALM SUNDAY

APRIL

s	m	t	w	t	f	s
					1	2
3	4	5	6	7	8	9
10	11	12	13	14	15	16
17	18	19	20	21	22	23
24	25	26	27	28	29	30

april

monday

18 ○

PASSOVER (BEGINS AT SUNSET)

tuesday

19

wednesday

20

april

GOOD FRIDAY
BANK HOLIDAY (CANADA, UK)
EARTH DAY

EASTER

APRIL

s	m	t	w	t	f	s
					1	2
3	4	5	6	7	8	9
10	11	12	13	14	15	16
17	18	19	20	21	22	23
24	25	26	27	28	29	30

april

monday
25 ◑

tuesday
26

wednesday
27

EASTER MONDAY (CANADA, UK EXCEPT SCOTLAND)

apr ▪ may

thursday
28 | 118

friday
29 | 119

saturday
30 | 120

sunday
1 | 121

MAY

s	m	t	w	t	f	s
1	2	3	4	5	6	7
8	9	10	11	12	13	14
15	16	17	18	19	20	21
22	23	24	25	26	27	28
29	30	31				

may

122

monday

2

BANK HOLIDAY (UK)

123

tuesday

3 ●

124

wednesday

4

may

thursday
CINCO DE MAYO

5 |125

friday

6 |126

saturday

7 |127

sunday
MOTHER'S DAY

8 |128

MAY

s	m	t	w	t	f	s
1	2	3	4	5	6	7
8	9	10	11	12	13	14
15	16	17	18	19	20	21
22	23	24	25	26	27	28
29	30	31				

may

monday
9

tuesday
10 ◐

wednesday
11

may

MAY

s	m	t	w	t	f	s
1	2	3	4	5	6	7
8	9	10	11	12	13	14
15	16	17	18	19	20	21
22	23	24	25	26	27	28
29	30	31				

may

monday

16

tuesday

17 ○

wednesday

18

may

ARMED FORCES DAY

MAY

s	m	t	w	t	f	s
1	2	3	4	5	6	7
8	9	10	11	12	13	14
15	16	17	18	19	20	21
22	23	24	25	26	27	28
29	30	31				

may

monday
23

VICTORIA DAY (CANADA)

tuesday
24 ◑

wednesday
25

may

thursday

26 | 146

friday

27 | 147

saturday

28 | 148

sunday

29 | 149

MAY

s	m	t	w	t	f	s
1	2	3	4	5	6	7
8	9	10	11	12	13	14
15	16	17	18	19	20	21
22	23	24	25	26	27	28
29	30	31				

may ▪ jun

MEMORIAL DAY
BANK HOLIDAY (UK)

june

JUNE

s	m	t	w	t	f	s
			1	2	3	4
5	6	7	8	9	10	11
12	13	14	15	16	17	18
19	20	21	22	23	24	25
26	27	28	29	30		

june

monday

6

157

tuesday

7

158

wednesday

8

159

june

thursday

◐ 9 | 160

friday

10 | 161

saturday

11 | 162

sunday

12 | 163

JUNE

s	m	t	w	t	f	s
			1	2	3	4
5	6	7	8	9	10	11
12	13	14	15	16	17	18
19	20	21	22	23	24	25
26	27	28	29	30		

june

monday
13

tuesday
14   **FLAG DAY**

wednesday
15 ○

june

thursday

16

167

friday

17

168

saturday

18

169

FATHER'S DAY

sunday

19

170

JUNE

s	m	t	w	t	f	s
			1	2	3	4
5	6	7	8	9	10	11
12	13	14	15	16	17	18
19	20	21	22	23	24	25
26	27	28	29	30		

june

monday
20

tuesday
21

SUMMER SOLSTICE 17:16 UTC

wednesday
22

june

thursday

◑ 23 | 174

friday

24 | 175

saturday

25 | 176

sunday

26 | 177

JUNE

s	m	t	w	t	f	s
			1	2	3	4
5	6	7	8	9	10	11
12	13	14	15	16	17	18
19	20	21	22	23	24	25
26	27	28	29	30		

june

monday
27

tuesday
28

wednesday
29

jun ▪ jul

CANADA DAY (CANADA)

JULY

s	m	t	w	t	f	s
					1	2
3	4	5	6	7	8	9
10	11	12	13	14	15	16
17	18	19	20	21	22	23
24	25	26	27	28	29	30
31						

july

july

JULY

s	m	t	w	t	f	s
					1	2
3	4	5	6	7	8	9
10	11	12	13	14	15	16
17	18	19	20	21	22	23
24	25	26	27	28	29	30
31						

july

monday
11

tuesday
12

BANK HOLIDAY (N. IRELAND)

wednesday
13

july

JULY

s	m	t	w	t	f	s
					1	2
3	4	5	6	7	8	9
10	11	12	13	14	15	16
17	18	19	20	21	22	23
24	25	26	27	28	29	30
31						

july

monday
18

tuesday
19

wednesday
20

july

JULY

s	m	t	w	t	f	s
					1	2
3	4	5	6	7	8	9
10	11	12	13	14	15	16
17	18	19	20	21	22	23
24	25	26	27	28	29	30
31						

july

monday
25

tuesday
26

wednesday
27

july

JULY

s	m	t	w	t	f	s
					1	2
3	4	5	6	7	8	9
10	11	12	13	14	15	16
17	18	19	20	21	22	23
24	25	26	27	28	29	30
31						

august

monday
1

CIVIC HOLIDAY (CANADA, MOST PROVINCES)
BANK HOLIDAY (SCOTLAND)

tuesday
2

wednesday
3

august

thursday

4 | 216

friday

5 | 217

saturday

◑ 6 | 218

sunday

7 | 219

AUGUST

s	m	t	w	t	f	s
	1	2	3	4	5	6
7	8	9	10	11	12	13
14	15	16	17	18	19	20
21	22	23	24	25	26	27
28	29	30	31			

august

| monday
8

| tuesday
9

| wednesday
10

august

AUGUST

s	m	t	w	t	f	s
	1	2	3	4	5	6
7	8	9	10	11	12	13
14	15	16	17	18	19	20
21	22	23	24	25	26	27
28	29	30	31			

august

monday
15

tuesday
16

wednesday
17

august

thursday
18 | 230

friday
19 | 231

saturday
20 | 232

sunday
◑ 21 | 233

AUGUST

s	m	t	w	t	f	s
	1	2	3	4	5	6
7	8	9	10	11	12	13
14	15	16	17	18	19	20
21	22	23	24	25	26	27
28	29	30	31			

august

monday
22

tuesday
23

wednesday
24

august

thursday
25
₂₃₇

friday
26
₂₃₈

saturday
27
₂₃₉

sunday
28
₂₄₀

AUGUST

s	m	t	w	t	f	s
	1	2	3	4	5	6
7	8	9	10	11	12	13
14	15	16	17	18	19	20
21	22	23	24	25	26	27
28	29	30	31			

august

monday

29 ●

BANK HOLIDAY (UK EXCEPT SCOTLAND)

tuesday

30

wednesday

31

september

thursday
1 | 244

friday
2 | 245

saturday
3 | 246

sunday
◑ 4 | 247

SEPTEMBER

s	m	t	w	t	f	s
				1	2	3
4	5	6	7	8	9	10
11	12	13	14	15	16	17
18	19	20	21	22	23	24
25	26	27	28	29	30	

september

monday
5
LABOR DAY (US, CANADA)

tuesday
6

wednesday
7

september

thursday

8 | 251

friday

9 | 252

saturday

10 | 253

sunday

11 | 254

SEPTEMBER

s	m	t	w	t	f	s
				1	2	3
4	5	6	7	8	9	10
11	12	13	14	15	16	17
18	19	20	21	22	23	24
25	26	27	28	29	30	

september

monday
12 ○

tuesday
13

wednesday
14

september

SEPTEMBER

s	m	t	w	t	f	s
				1	2	3
4	5	6	7	8	9	10
11	12	13	14	15	16	17
18	19	20	21	22	23	24
25	26	27	28	29	30	

september

INTERNATIONAL DAY OF PEACE

september

thursday
22
265

AUTUMNAL EQUINOX 09:04 UTC

friday
23
266

saturday
24
267

sunday
25
268

SEPTEMBER

s	m	t	w	t	f	s
				1	2	3
4	5	6	7	8	9	10
11	12	13	14	15	16	17
18	19	20	21	22	23	24
25	26	27	28	29	30	

september

monday
26

tuesday
27 ●

wednesday
28   ROSH HASHANAH (BEGINS AT SUNSET)

sep ▪ oct

OCTOBER

s	m	t	w	t	f	s
						1
2	3	4	5	6	7	8
9	10	11	12	13	14	15
16	17	18	19	20	21	22
23	24	25	26	27	28	29
30	31					

october

monday
3

tuesday
4 ◑

wednesday
5

october

YOM KIPPUR (BEGINS AT SUNSET)

OCTOBER

s	m	t	w	t	f	s
						1
2	3	4	5	6	7	8
9	10	11	12	13	14	15
16	17	18	19	20	21	22
23	24	25	26	27	28	29
30	31					

october

monday
10

COLUMBUS DAY
THANKSGIVING DAY (CANADA)

tuesday
11

wednesday
12 ○

october

OCTOBER

s	m	t	w	t	f	s
						1
2	3	4	5	6	7	8
9	10	11	12	13	14	15
16	17	18	19	20	21	22
23	24	25	26	27	28	29
30	31					

october

monday
17

tuesday
18

wednesday
19

october

OCTOBER

s	m	t	w	t	f	s
						1
2	3	4	5	6	7	8
9	10	11	12	13	14	15
16	17	18	19	20	21	22
23	24	25	26	27	28	29
30	31					

october

monday

24

UNITED NATIONS DAY

tuesday

25

wednesday

26 ●

october

SUMMER TIME ENDS (UK)

OCTOBER

s	m	t	w	t	f	s
						1
2	3	4	5	6	7	8
9	10	11	12	13	14	15
16	17	18	19	20	21	22
23	24	25	26	27	28	29
30	31					

oct ▪ nov

monday

31

HALLOWEEN

304

tuesday

1

305

wednesday

2

306

november

DAYLIGHT SAVING TIME ENDS

NOVEMBER

s	m	t	w	t	f	s
		1	2	3	4	5
6	7	8	9	10	11	12
13	14	15	16	17	18	19
20	21	22	23	24	25	26
27	28	29	30			

november

monday
7

tuesday
8

wednesday
9

november

VETERANS DAY
REMEMBRANCE DAY (CANADA)

NOVEMBER

s	m	t	w	t	f	s
		1	2	3	4	5
6	7	8	9	10	11	12
13	14	15	16	17	18	19
20	21	22	23	24	25	26
27	28	29	30			

november

monday
14

tuesday
15

wednesday
16

november

NOVEMBER

s	m	t	w	t	f	s
		1	2	3	4	5
6	7	8	9	10	11	12
13	14	15	16	17	18	19
20	21	22	23	24	25	26
27	28	29	30			

november

monday
21

tuesday
22

wednesday
23

november

THANKSGIVING

NOVEMBER

s	m	t	w	t	f	s
		1	2	3	4	5
6	7	8	9	10	11	12
13	14	15	16	17	18	19
20	21	22	23	24	25	26
27	28	29	30			

november

332 *monday*
28

333 *tuesday*
29

334 *wednesday*
30

ST. ANDREW'S DAY (SCOTLAND)

december

DECEMBER

s	m	t	w	t	f	s
				1	2	3
4	5	6	7	8	9	10
11	12	13	14	15	16	17
18	19	20	21	22	23	24
25	26	27	28	29	30	31

december

monday
5

tuesday
6

wednesday
7

december

DECEMBER

s	m	t	w	t	f	s
				1	2	3
4	5	6	7	8	9	10
11	12	13	14	15	16	17
18	19	20	21	22	23	24
25	26	27	28	29	30	31

december

monday
12

tuesday
13

wednesday
14

december

DECEMBER

s	m	t	w	t	f	s
				1	2	3
4	5	6	7	8	9	10
11	12	13	14	15	16	17
18	19	20	21	22	23	24
25	26	27	28	29	30	31

december

monday
19

tuesday
20

HANUKKAH (BEGINS AT SUNSET)

wednesday
21

december

WINTER SOLSTICE 05:30 UTC

thursday
22 | 356

friday
23 | 357

saturday
● 24 | 358

CHRISTMAS

sunday
25 | 359

DECEMBER

s	m	t	w	t	f	s
				1	2	3
4	5	6	7	8	9	10
11	12	13	14	15	16	17
18	19	20	21	22	23	24
25	26	27	28	29	30	31

december

monday

26

CHRISTMAS HOLIDAY
KWANZAA BEGINS
BOXING DAY (CANADA, UK)

tuesday

27

BANK HOLIDAY (UK)

wednesday

28

dec ▪ jan

thursday
29 | 363

friday
30 | 364

saturday
31 | 365

NEW YEAR'S DAY

sunday
◗ 1 | 1

JANUARY

s	m	t	w	t	f	s
1	2	3	4	5	6	7
8	9	10	11	12	13	14
15	16	17	18	19	20	21
22	23	24	25	26	27	28
29	30	31				

2011 INTERNATIONAL HOLIDAYS

Following are the dates of major holidays in 2011 for selected countries. Islamic observances are subject to adjustment. Holidays of the United States, United Kingdom, and Canada, and major Jewish holidays, appear on this calendar's grid pages. Pomegranate is not responsible for errors or omissions in this list. Users of this information should confirm dates with local sources before making international travel or business plans. Please note: Most international holidays that fall on a weekend are observed on the following Monday (or the next working day).

ARGENTINA
1	Jan	New Year's Day
24	Mar	National Day of Memory for Truth and Justice
2	Apr	Veterans Day (Malvinas War Memorial)
21	Apr	Holy Thursday
22	Apr	Good Friday
24	Apr	Easter
1	May	Labor Day
25	May	Revolution Day
20	Jun	Flag Day*
9	Jul	Independence Day
15	Aug	San Martín Day*
12	Oct	Día de la Diversidad Cultural Americana†
8	Dec	Immaculate Conception
25	Dec	Christmas

* Observed on third Monday of month
† Observed on second Monday of October

AUSTRALIA
1	Jan	New Year's Day
26	Jan	Australia Day
7	Mar	Labor Day (WA)
14	Mar	Labor Day (Vic)
		Eight Hours Day (Tas)
		Adelaide Cup (SA)
		Canberra Day (ACT)
22-25	Apr	Easter Holiday
26	Apr	ANZAC Day
		Easter Tuesday (Tas)
2	May	Labor Day (Qld)
		May Day (NT)
6	Jun	Foundation Day (WA)
13	Jun	Queen's Birthday (except WA)
		Volunteer's Day (SA)
1	Aug	Picnic Day (NT)
		Bank Holiday (NSW)
3	Oct	Queen's Birthday (WA)
		Labor Day (NSW, ACT, SA)
1	Nov	Melbourne Cup (Vic)
25	Dec	Christmas
26	Dec	Boxing Day (except SA)
		Christmas Holiday (SA)
27	Dec	Proclamation Day (SA)

BRAZIL
1	Jan	New Year's Day
20	Jan	Sao Sebastião Day (Rio de Janeiro)
25	Jan	São Paulo Anniversary (São Paulo)
7-8	Mar	Carnival
9	Mar	Ash Wednesday (until 2 pm)
21	Apr	Tiradentes Day
22	Apr	Good Friday
24	Apr	Easter
1	May	Labor Day
23	Jun	Corpus Christi
7	Sep	Independence Day
12	Oct	Our Lady of Aparecida

2	Nov	All Souls' Day
15	Nov	Proclamation of the Republic
25	Dec	Christmas

CHINA (SEE ALSO HONG KONG)
1	Jan	New Year's Day
2	Feb	Chinese New Year Holiday begins
8	Feb	Last Day of New Year Holiday
5	Apr	Tomb-Sweeping Day
1	May	Labor Day
6	Jun	Dragon Boat Festival
12	Sep	Mid-Autumn Festival
26 Sep-2 Oct		National Day Holiday

FRANCE
1	Jan	New Year's Day
24	Apr	Easter
25	Apr	Easter Monday
1	May	Labor Day
8	May	Victory in Europe Day
2	Jun	Ascension Day
12	Jun	Pentecost
13	Jun	Whit Monday
14	Jul	Bastille Day
15	Aug	Assumption
1	Nov	All Saints' Day
11	Nov	Armistice Day
25	Dec	Christmas

GERMANY
1	Jan	New Year's Day
22	Apr	Good Friday
24	Apr	Easter
25	Apr	Easter Monday
1	May	Labor Day
2	Jun	Ascension Day
12	Jun	Pentecost
13	Jun	Whit Monday
3	Oct	Unity Day
25	Dec	Christmas
26	Dec	St. Stephen's Day

HONG KONG
1	Jan	New Year's Day
3-5	Feb	Spring Festival / Lunar New Year
2-5	Apr	Easter Holiday
5	Apr	Tomb-Sweeping Day
22	Apr	Good Friday
23	Apr	Holy Saturday
24	Apr	Easter
25	Apr	Easter Monday
1	May	Labor Day
10	May	Buddha's Birthday
6	Jun	Dragon Boat Festival
1	Jul	Special Administrative Region Establishment Day
13	Sep	Day After Mid-Autumn Festival
1	Oct	National Day
5	Oct	Chung Yeung Festival
25	Dec	Christmas
26	Dec	Boxing Day

INDIA
1	Jan	New Year's Day
14	Jan	Makar Sankranti (North India)
15	Jan	Makar Sankranti (Bengal)
26	Jan	Republic Day
15	Feb	Prophet Muhammad's Birthday
16	Feb	Milad-un-Nabi
3	Mar	Maha Shivaratri
19	Mar	Holi
12	Apr	Ram Navami
14	Apr	Dr. B. R. Ambedkar's Birthday
16	Apr	Mahavir Jayanti
22	Apr	Good Friday
24	Apr	Easter
17	May	Buddha Purnima
15	Aug	Independence Day
21	Aug	Janamashtami
31	Aug	Ramzan-Eid (Eid al-Fitr)
2	Oct	Mahatma Gandhi's Birthday
26	Oct	Diwali (Deepavali)
7	Nov	Bakr-Eid (Eid al-Adha)
11	Nov	Guru Nanak's Birthday
6	Dec	Islamic New Year
25	Dec	Christmas

IRELAND
1	Jan	New Year's Day
17	Mar	St. Patrick's Day
22	Apr	Good Friday
24	Apr	Easter
25	Apr	Easter Monday
2	May	Bank Holiday
6	Jun	Bank Holiday
1	Aug	Bank Holiday
31	Oct	Bank Holiday
25	Dec	Christmas
26	Dec	St. Stephen's Day

ISRAEL
20	Mar	Purim (except Jerusalem)
21	Mar	Purim Bank Holiday (Jerusalem)
19	Apr	First Day of Pesach
25	Apr	Last Day of Pesach
1	May	Holocaust Memorial Day
9	May	National Memorial Day
10	May	Independence Day
8	Jun	Shavuot
9	Aug	Tisha B'Av
29-30	Sep	Rosh Hashanah
8	Oct	Yom Kippur
13	Oct	First Day of Sukkot
20	Oct	Shemini Atzeret / Simhat Torah

ITALY
1	Jan	New Year's Day
6	Jan	Epiphany
24	Apr	Easter
25	Apr	Easter Monday
		Liberation Day
1	May	Labor Day
2	Jun	Republic Day
29	Jun	Sts. Peter and Paul (Rome)

15	Aug	Assumption
1	Nov	All Saints' Day
8	Dec	Immaculate Conception
25	Dec	Christmas
26	Dec	St. Stephen's Day

JAPAN

1	Jan	New Year's Day
10	Jan	Coming of Age Day
11	Feb	National Foundation Day
21	Mar	Vernal Equinox
29	Apr	Shōwa Day
3	May	Constitution Memorial Day
4	May	Greenery Day
5	May	Children's Day
18	Jul	Marine Day
19	Sep	Respect for the Aged Day
23	Sep	Autumnal Equinox
10	Oct	Health and Sports Day
3	Nov	Culture Day
23	Nov	Labor Thanksgiving Day
23	Dec	Emperor's Birthday

MEXICO

1	Jan	New Year's Day
5	Feb	Constitution Day*
21	Mar	Benito Juárez Day†
21	Apr	Holy Thursday
22	Apr	Good Friday
24	Apr	Easter
1	May	Labor Day
16	Sep	Independence Day
1	Nov	All Saints' Day
2	Nov	All Souls' Day (Day of the Dead)
20	Nov	Revolution Day†
12	Dec	Our Lady of Guadalupe
25	Dec	Christmas

* Observed on first Monday of month
† Observed on third Monday of month

NETHERLANDS

1	Jan	New Year's Day
22	Apr	Good Friday
24	Apr	Easter
25	Apr	Easter Monday
30	Apr	Queen's Day
2	Jun	Ascension Day
12	Jun	Pentecost
13	Jun	Whit Monday
25-26	Dec	Christmas Holiday

NEW ZEALAND

1-2	Jan	New Year's Holiday
22	Jan	Provincial Anniversary (Wellington)*
29	Jan	Provincial Anniversary (Auckland)*
6	Feb	Waitangi Day
22	Apr	Good Friday
24	Apr	Easter
25	Apr	Easter Monday
		ANZAC Day
6	Jun	Queen's Birthday
24	Oct	Labor Day
11	Nov	Provincial Anniversary (Canterbury)
25	Dec	Christmas
26	Dec	Boxing Day

* Observed on closest Monday

PUERTO RICO

6	Jan	Three Kings Day (Epiphany)
11	Jan	Eugenio María de Hostos Day*
22	Mar	Emancipation Day
16	Apr	José de Diego Day†
22	Apr	Good Friday
24	Apr	Easter
17	Jul	Luis Muñoz Rivera Day†
25	Jul	Constitution Day
27	Jul	José Celso Barbosa Day
12	Oct	Día de la Raza*
19	Nov	Discovery of Puerto Rico
24	Dec	Christmas Eve

All US federal holidays also observed
* Observed on second Monday of month
† Observed on third Monday of month

RUSSIA

3	Jan	New Year's Holiday Begins
7	Jan	Orthodox Christmas
10	Jan	Last Day of New Year's Holiday
23	Feb	Defenders of the Fatherland Day
8	Mar	International Women's Day
24	Apr	Orthodox Easter
1	May	Spring and Labor Day
9	May	Victory Day
12	Jun	Independence Day
4	Nov	National Unity Day

SINGAPORE

1	Jan	New Year's Day
3-4	Feb	Chinese New Year Holiday
22	Apr	Good Friday
24	Apr	Easter
1	May	Labor Day
17	May	Vesak Day (Buddha's Birthday)
31	Jul	Beginning of Ramadan
9	Aug	National Day
29	Aug	Hari Raya Puasa (Eid al-Fitr)
26	Oct	Deepavali
5	Nov	Hari Raya Haji (Eid al-Adha)
25	Dec	Christmas

SOUTH AFRICA

1	Jan	New Year's Day
21	Mar	Human Rights Day
22	Apr	Good Friday
24	Apr	Easter
25	Apr	Family Day
27	Apr	Freedom Day
1	May	Workers' Day
16	Jun	Youth Day
9	Aug	National Women's Day
24	Sep	Heritage Day
16	Dec	Day of Reconciliation
25	Dec	Christmas
26	Dec	Day of Goodwill

SOUTH KOREA

1	Jan	New Year's Day
2-4	Feb	Lunar New Year Holiday
1	Mar	Independence Movement Day
5	May	Children's Day
10	May	Birth of Buddha
6	Jun	Memorial Day
17	Jul	Constitution Day
15	Aug	Independence Day
11-13	Sep	Harvest Moon Festival
3	Oct	National Foundation Day
25	Dec	Christmas

SPAIN

1	Jan	New Year's Day
6	Jan	Epiphany
21	Apr	Holy Thursday
22	Apr	Good Friday
24	Apr	Easter
1	May	Labor Day
15	Aug	Assumption
12	Oct	National Day
1	Nov	All Saints' Day
6	Dec	Constitution Day
8	Dec	Immaculate Conception
25	Dec	Christmas

SWEDEN

1	Jan	New Year's Day
5	Jan	Epiphany Eve
6	Jan	Epiphany
21	Apr	Maundy Thursday
22	Apr	Good Friday
24	Apr	Easter
25	Apr	Easter Monday
30	Apr	Walpurgis Eve
		King's Birthday
1	May	May Day
1	Jun	Day Before Ascension
2	Jun	Ascension Day
6	Jun	National Day
12	Jun	Pentecost
24	Jun	Midsummer Eve
25	Jun	Midsummer Day
4	Nov	All Saints' Eve
5	Nov	All Saints' Day
24	Dec	Christmas Eve
25	Dec	Christmas
26	Dec	Boxing Day
31	Dec	New Year's Eve

SWITZERLAND

1	Jan	New Year's Day
22	Apr	Good Friday
24	Apr	Easter
25	Apr	Easter Monday
2	Jun	Ascension Day
12	Jun	Pentecost
13	Jun	Whit Monday
1	Aug	National Day
25	Dec	Christmas

THAILAND

1	Jan	New Year's Day
18	Feb	Makha Bucha Day
6	Apr	Chakri Day
13-15	Apr	Songkran (Thai New Year)
1	May	Labor Day
5	May	Coronation Day
17	May	Visakha Bucha Day (Buddha's Birthday)
15	Jul	Asanha Bucha Day
16	Jul	Khao Phansa (Buddhist Lent begins)
12	Aug	Queen's Birthday
23	Oct	Chulalongkorn Day
10	Nov	Loy Kratong
5	Dec	King's Birthday
10	Dec	Constitution Day
31	Dec	New Year's Eve

WORLD TIME ZONE MAP

This map is based on Coordinated Universal Time (UTC), the worldwide system of civil timekeeping. UTC is essentially equivalent to Greenwich Mean Time. Zone boundaries are approximate and subject to change. Time differences relative to UTC shown here are based on the use of standard time; where Daylight Saving Time (Summer Time) is employed, add one hour to local standard time.

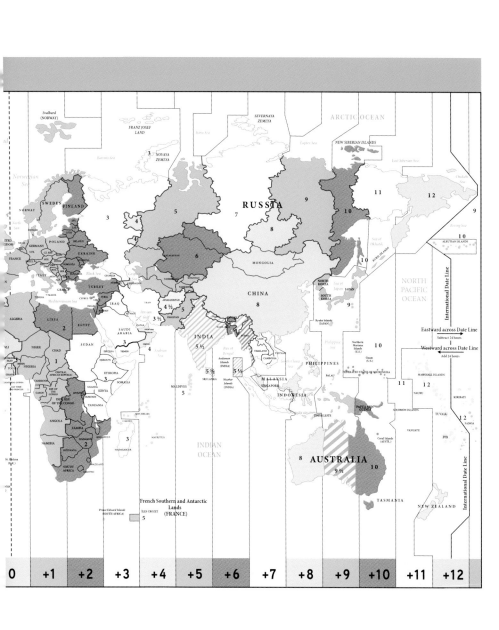

2012

JANUARY

s	m	t	w	t	f	s
1	2	3	4	5	6	7
8	9	10	11	12	13	14
15	16	17	18	19	20	21
22	23	24	25	26	27	28
29	30	31				

FEBRUARY

s	m	t	w	t	f	s
			1	2	3	4
5	6	7	8	9	10	11
12	13	14	15	16	17	18
19	20	21	22	23	24	25
26	27	28	29			

MARCH

s	m	t	w	t	f	s
				1	2	3
4	5	6	7	8	9	10
11	12	13	14	15	16	17
18	19	20	21	22	23	24
25	26	27	28	29	30	31

APRIL

s	m	t	w	t	f	s
1	2	3	4	5	6	7
8	9	10	11	12	13	14
15	16	17	18	19	20	21
22	23	24	25	26	27	28
29	30					

MAY

s	m	t	w	t	f	s
		1	2	3	4	5
6	7	8	9	10	11	12
13	14	15	16	17	18	19
20	21	22	23	24	25	26
27	28	29	30	31		

JUNE

s	m	t	w	t	f	s
					1	2
3	4	5	6	7	8	9
10	11	12	13	14	15	16
17	18	19	20	21	22	23
24	25	26	27	28	29	30

2012

JULY

s	m	t	w	t	f	s
1	2	3	4	5	6	7
8	9	10	11	12	13	14
15	16	17	18	19	20	21
22	23	24	25	26	27	28
29	30	31				

AUGUST

s	m	t	w	t	f	s
			1	2	3	4
5	6	7	8	9	10	11
12	13	14	15	16	17	18
19	20	21	22	23	24	25
26	27	28	29	30	31	

SEPTEMBER

s	m	t	w	t	f	s
						1
2	3	4	5	6	7	8
9	10	11	12	13	14	15
16	17	18	19	20	21	22
23	24	25	26	27	28	29
30						

OCTOBER

s	m	t	w	t	f	s
	1	2	3	4	5	6
7	8	9	10	11	12	13
14	15	16	17	18	19	20
21	22	23	24	25	26	27
28	29	30	31			

NOVEMBER

s	m	t	w	t	f	s
				1	2	3
4	5	6	7	8	9	10
11	12	13	14	15	16	17
18	19	20	21	22	23	24
25	26	27	28	29	30	

DECEMBER

s	m	t	w	t	f	s
						1
2	3	4	5	6	7	8
9	10	11	12	13	14	15
16	17	18	19	20	21	22
23	24	25	26	27	28	29
30	31					

Notes

Notes

BKliban ®

Personal Information

name _____

address _____

city _____ state _____ zip _____

phone _____

cell/pgr _____ fax _____

e-mail _____

in case of emergency, please notify:

name _____

address _____

city _____ state _____ zip _____

phone _____

physician's name _____

physician's phone _____

health insurance company _____

plan number _____

allergies _____

other _____

driver's license number _____

car insurance company _____

policy number _____